More Time, Gentlemen, Please.

Designed by Alan Waldie
Written by Peter Mayle
Inspired by thirst and Anthony Simonds-Gooding

First published 1984 by
André Deutsch Limited
105 Great Russell Street, London WC1

Printed in Great Britain by
Biddles of Guildford, Surrey

ISBN 0 233 97740 6

More Time, Gentlemen, Please.

by
Peter Mayle

Required reading for beer fanciers, darts players and all our honourable friends in the House of Commons

INCLUDING
NUMEROUS ARTISTIC CONTRIBUTIONS
From England's top cartoonists.

ANDRE DEUTSCH

Merry England, 1915-1984.

For nearly 70 years now, our drinking habits have been governed by the clock. If someone suggests a drink, the first thing you do is look at your watch. It's a national reflex.

But the innocent tourist, thirsty for culture and sometimes for beer, is in for a dry old time if he doesn't know the rules. Visitors to our damp island are constantly finding patches of drought where they least expect to find them: in our pubs. And one of the most poignant sights of the tourist season is the bewildered group of Americans, dusty and parched after rummaging through the British Museum, with their noses pressed up against the window of The Goat in Gaiters at four in the afternoon.

They confer. Well, it sure *looks* like a bar. Maybe there's another entrance. They circle the premises until a passer-by takes pity on them and tells them to come back at 5:30. The news is greeted with a mixture of irritation and disbelief – *you're kidding!* – but reluctantly accepted as further evidence of our eccentric nature; another quaint English tradition like Beefeaters and underheated bedrooms.

In fact, it isn't a tradition at all, but the world's longest-running emergency measure.

Apart from a short dry spell some 500 years ago, when ale houses were shut down to get the army back to its archery practice, the English tradition was to have a drink when you felt like it.

This stopped in 1915. Curiously enough, the 1915 restrictions, like the mediaeval ones, were designed to divert our attentions from a quiet pint to more warlike matters. The government of the day, suspecting that the charms of the pub outweighed those of an armaments factory, imposed time limits on the public sale of intoxicating drink. Munitions workers were obliged to take their refreshment between set hours: 11:00 to 2:00 and 5:30 to 10:30.

The armaments were duly made. War was concluded, peace came, the emergency went, and the restrictions stayed.

And they're still here, despite circumstances and society having changed out of all recognition since 1915. Although, of course, as with all restrictions, there are ways round them.

You can, for instance, go into a supermarket at nine in the morning and buy all the drink you can carry. In Boots the Chemist, just a short walk from the corn plasters and disposable nappies, you will find everything you need for a do-it-yourself brewery, as well as a selection of winemaking kits.

You can join a private club and have a gin and tonic at teatime. You can have beer with your breakfast on a train, Scotch at midnight on a plane, and almost anything at almost any time on a boat – the one condition being that you may only drink legally when these forms of transport are moving. The law offers no precise guidance as to what you should do if your train is stuck outside Birmingham for half an hour. (Dare you risk a stationary sip? Should you wait until the train moves off? Are the penalties more severe than for using the lavatory while the train is standing in a station?) But then no law can cover all eventualities.

If none of these loopholes appeals to you, consider a career in politics. The Mother of Parliaments looks with sympathy on those who serve her, and her drinking hours are, to say the least, flexible. It is comforting to know that our elected representatives, God bless 'em, are not deprived of social amenities simply because they work irregular hours. When they come off the night shift – a debate, let us say, where the cut and thrust has continued into the small hours of the morning – it is not unknown for them to feel like a quick one. And why not? Legislating is thirsty work, and cannot always be concluded in neat, nine to five time slots.

Consequently, the House of Commons bar, sometimes known as The Division Bell Arms, is open for business whenever the House is in session. A shining example of how minority needs can be catered for in a democratic society.

So, one way or another, it *is* technically possible to have a drink outside the prescribed hours as long as you don't want to go to a pub to have it.

There is, however, one fairly recent and very interesting exception to all this – a place where the clock is more accommodating, and where an afternoon drink does not have to be taken in a private club or in motion. It is Scotland.

DARTS
TONIGHT
SNAKEBITE ARMS
-V-
WHITE LION
TEAMS-
BAGGY SHORT-SLEEVED SHINY SHIRTS ONLY PLEASE
OF COURSE, I'M ONLY A SOCIAL DRINKER MYSELF.
M
IT W
MAGI
ADDED
CONFID
GREATE

O - I FIND
S LIKE
GIVE YOU
ISE, SELF
E AND
PULARITY.
FIFTY PINTS OF LAGER PLEASE STUART, AND ONE FOR YOUR GOOD SELF.
Pork Scratchings
PIG
PIG
PIG
PIG
NUTS
Menu
BIFF.

Law and order north of the border.

"Occasional and regular extensions of the permitted hours."

This ringing phrase became law in Scotland on July 1st, 1977. Since then, it has been possible for pubs to stay open from 11 in the morning until 11 at night, or even later. Licensed hotels and restaurants can open at 11, and stay open until 1:30 the following morning, with a half hour break in the afternoon.

Not earth-shattering changes, by any means. Nevertheless, they didn't escape criticism. Grave reservations were expressed. Doubting Hamish and his friends made gloomy forecasts. And amid the general rumblings about whisky galore and bands of revellers roaming the streets at all hours, there were several specific worries:

- Would the level of alcoholism increase?
- Would performance at work be affected?
- Would there be outbreaks of public mischief?
- Would there be a higher incidence of drink and drive offences?
- Would the police be able to cope?
- Did the publican want to work longer hours?
- Did the public want to drink longer hours?

Nobody would argue that these are not very proper and responsible concerns, put forward by well-meaning people who probably like the odd drink themselves. But certain subjects - from sex, politics and individual liberty to a blind faith in the local football team - provoke reactions that are often based on instinct as much as reason. Alcohol is one of these delicate matters; you and I can handle our enjoyment in moderation, but what about the rest of them? Heaven knows what might happen if *they* were let loose in pubs for twelve hours a day.

Before we see what actually did happen, it's worth looking at the way in which the changed laws were designed to operate.

Let's start behind the bar. The new laws were not introduced to twist the publican's arm into pulling more pints. He wasn't under any legal obligation to extend his opening hours. If, in his judgement, his customers wanted the extra time – and providing he was prepared to do the extra work – he could apply for the newly-extended hours. If not, he carried on as before.

If he wanted longer hours for one day a week, to put the darts team through their aerobic exercises, he applied for a once-a-week extension.

If he wanted to stay open for longer on Saturdays, market days, his wedding anniversary, or Bonnie Prince Charlie's birthday, he could apply for special extensions. But he didn't have to.

In other words, the laws were those of permission rather than imposition. They were flexible. They allowed for a wide variety of local circumstances and individual needs. They were there to be used if required, on the old principle of supply and demand.

Along with the new laws came a new system to administer them – District Licensing Boards whose purpose was to safeguard the common interest, nip any hints of wretched excess in the bud, keep an eye out for that vaguely defined anti-social malady called public nuisance, and generally see fair play. Anyone who was previously entitled to object to any aspect of a licence could still do so under the new arrangements, and the penalties for renegade licence holders were just as severe as they had always been. Woe betide the publican who put his own elastic interpretation on the law. He would be fined, stripped of his licence and drummed out of the pub. A fate, for those in the business, worse than bankruptcy.

So far, then, everything was orderly and more or less predictable. But now we come to the Great Unknown, the mystery element that caused a modest change in legislation to be looked upon as a social experiment, the one factor that wouldn't fit neatly into a pre-arranged system of controls: the many-headed monster with a raging thirst. Yes indeed. The Scottish public. And this is where the worries of the worriers shifted into overdrive.

The men and women of Scotland, as they themselves will cheerfully admit, are on good terms with drink. Hard winters encourage a taste for soft, smoky whisky, and the Scot is not a man to be trifled with when he is attending to his beer. Give him several extra hours of drinking time, said the pessimists, and there you have a recipe for Hogmanay every night. Madness! In extreme cases, the level of alarm was similar to that recorded by Robert Burns as he observed the mouse he later wrote about:

"O, what a panic's in thy breastie!"

But what may have been overlooked by those with panic in their breasties is the simple and sometimes disagreeable fact that you can't drink on an empty wallet.

Leaving aside for the moment such personal considerations as depth of thirst and hardness of head, the main influence on our drinking is not time, but cash. Most of us have a limited amount of money to spend in the pub, and most of us go to the pub for social as well as alcoholic reasons. It follows that if you want to spend more time with your friends without a corresponding increase in your drinking budget, you will have to stretch the budget. Your consumption stays the same, but you take longer to consume it.

The WHETTED PALATE
Licensed to make Life Difficult.
PRIV
PUB
HOU
Wines
Go
somewhere
ELSE
John Glashan

It's no use BEGGING — we're SHUT.
UP TIME
The ALWAYS CLOSED tavern
The NEVER OPEN TAVERN
But my wife's DYING for a drink ...

At any rate, that was the theory put forward by supporters of the new laws.

Now, with the benefit of more than seven years of hindsight, it's possible to see some results, count a few of the votes that have come in, and draw one or two conclusions.

The Pub.

There are more than 4,300 pubs in Scotland, and not all of them took advantage of the longer hours. Many of those that did were surprised to find that while their drink sales remained steady, they sold a lot more *food*. Late breakfasts and afternoon teas were added to the menu. And because of the extra time available, it was possible to offer a wider choice of food in the evenings. People coming out of the cinema, for example, could have a meal instead of trying to cram down a hasty sausage and a pint in the space of three and half minutes.

The Publican.

Longer hours and more work don't appear to have put him off. In 1978, the latest year for which figures are available, 69,927 special extensions were granted. Every one of these extensions had to be applied for by the publican, as a matter of personal choice.

More recently, a survey carried out in 1983 showed that 82 per cent of publicans preferred the new licensing system to the old one. A third of them claimed to be selling more food; nearly half of them said they had more customers but less drunkenness. The general view from behind the bar is that people are drinking about the same amount as they used to, but taking longer to do it.

Meanwhile, back in the House of Lords, the news is that:

> *"... surveys in March 1977 and November 1978 indicated that there was no significant change in the average consumption of alcohol, since those drinking tended to do so at a more leisurely pace."*
>
> – Lord Mansfield, April 25, 1983.

"...statistics have shown that consumption has actually decreased slightly, and so has street drunkenness."

Lord St. John of Bletso, May 9th, 1983.

The Public.

Scottish drinkers, it seems, are hardly going overboard as a result of extra drinking time. Even their attitudes, taken from another 1983 survey, are moderate. The majority of them (62 per cent) approve of the changed licensing laws, and there is general agreement that they have made pubs more pleasant, more suitable for women drinkers, more civilized, more likely to serve good food, less frantic at closing time, and more convenient: *"People work flexible hours so they should be able to drink flexible hours."*

Drinking and Driving.

"I am able to say that there has been no significant increase in drunkenness offences or motor vehicle offences caused through drink since the 1976 Act come into force."

That was Lord Lyell, speaking on behalf of the Government on June 18th, 1982. In other remarks made then, his Lordship confirmed that the Government had not received *"any representation that the increased hours have had any adverse effects."*

No adverse effects? None? Quite remarkable. If that's true – and who are we to doubt the noble Lord – and if the public likes the extended hours, why don't we try the same thing in England?

A good question. And one which, as we shall see, has been asked before.

Lessons from the good old days: Prohibition and the six o'clock swill.

Questions have often been asked in high places over the years about the suitability of our licensing laws. Once in a while, there is an encouraging response.

In 1971, the Home Secretary decided that the time was ripe for a review of the situation, and set up a Committee on Liquor Licensing, under the Chairmanship of Lord Erroll of Hale. The Committee went away, did its homework, and returned the following year. Its report was unanimous, which in itself is a little unusual; committees and unanimity don't always go together.

The main conclusions of the Erroll Report were these:

- *There was an impressive weight of opinion in favour of changing the law.*
- *Changes in leisure habits would require greater flexibility from licensed premises.*
- *Modest changes in the law would be unlikely to affect some of the deeper social causes of public drunkenness.*

One specific recommendation was that licensed premises should be permitted – but not compelled – to stay open at any time between 10 a.m. and midnight.

One can imagine the meeting that took place to consider the findings.

Well, gentlemen, where do we go from here? We appointed the members of the Committee. They have done their job thoroughly and well. The recommendations are unanimous. It seems like a cut and dried case for doing...what?

Did someone say absolutely nothing? Excellent idea. Let's do that.

And nothing is what was done.

The reasons for this inactivity, which has now lasted through thirteen years and four changes in Government, are not at all clear. There are, obviously, organisations and individuals who are opposed to any relaxation of our drinking laws. Their motives are sincere, and they are open in their arguments. But do they represent general public opinion? Probably not. Do they have the influence to stonewall the recommendations of an officially appointed committee? Again, probably not.

So we're left to speculate. *Why* has nothing happened? Has someone thrown a spanner in the works? What kind of spanner is it?

There are a number of possibilities, but one seems more likely that the rest. It is the old instinctive shudder of horror which ripples through the ranks of lawmakers whenever the ticklish question of alcohol and the common public comes up. It's nothing new. Nor is it confined to England. It's a belief – or maybe just a dark suspicion – that the man in the street, given the time and the opportunity, will go out and get swivel-eyed, snarling drunk, forsaking work, decency and the bosom of his family for the glass in his hand.

If this suspicion is correct, then surely the prudent thing to do is to restrict his drinking time, because the less time he has to drink, the less he will drink. Followed to its logical conclusion – if he has no time to drink, he will drink nothing – this argument leads to Prohibition. As it did in America.

When it was introduced in 1920, President Hoover

It isn't easy to break the habits of a lifetime...

called Prohibition a noble experiment. News pictures of the time show Federal Agents smiling broadly as they poured away thousands of barrels of liquor. America the Teetotal was launched on a sea of discarded drink.

It sank almost immediately. While the Feds were closing down bars, the bootleggers were opening up new ones. Amateur brewers and distillers mixed evil concoctions in their bathtubs. A line of boats stretched from Maine down to Florida, offering refreshment to anyone prepared to venture beyond the three-mile limit. Al Capone employed 700 men, and controlled 10,000 speakeasies. People carried liquor around in hip flasks, false books, hot water bottles, garden hosepipes and babies' prams. Smugglers imported well-known brands, watered them down and sold them on. Criminals became multi-millionaires, and vice versa. The senator who introduced the law was caught with a private still which produced 130 gallons of whiskey a day. In New York City alone, there were 100,000 illegal clubs and bars. Americans actually drank more than before.

Noble or not, the experiment was a flop.

There have been less drastic experiments, and less spectacular flops. But, try as one might to find an exception to the general pattern, drinking restrictions never seem to have the desired effect. They don't reduce drinking; they just speed it up. A man in search of refreshment will perform extraordinary feats of co-ordination between his right arm and his oesophagus if he is pressed for time, easily accelerating from nought to ten pints in less than an hour.

Legendary examples of high-velocity drinking used to be regular features of Australian social life. In many parts of Australia, pubs used to close at 6 p.m. If you finished work at five, and if you were fast on your feet, you might be able to get a few down before closing time, and it was these conditions that were reponsible for Australia's world domination in beat-the-clock drinking. As the minutes ticked away, drinkers braced themselves for the six o'clock swill – those final frenzied moments when glasses were filled and emptied almost too fast for the eye to follow, and certainly too fast for the digestive tract to cope with. The results were often unsavoury; what went down had to come up, disturbing the peace of the early evening and causing many a hangover before dinner time.

The law has now changed. In most states you can get a drink when you feel like it, which represents an increase in drinking time of several hundred per cent. According to the rules of pessimistic logic, this should have led to a similar increase in alcohol abuse, and in the number of moaning figures holding their heads at closing time.

It hasn't happened. Consumption has certainly gone up in the last thirty years (by 54 per cent, compared with 86 per cent in the U.K.), but anyone going to Australia expecting to find scenes of wild colonial debauch on every street corner will be disappointed. Australians are merely spreading their drinking over a longer period and undoubtedly enjoying it more as a result. A similar story, in that respect, to Scotland.

The lessons of alcoholic history are supported by alcoholic geography. For some reason, the colder the climate, the harsher the drinking restrictions are; countries in the northern vodka belt are famous for making it as difficult as possible to get a drink. But somehow, it doesn't seem to work.

Sweden, for instance, has a grand total of 316 liquor outlets to cater for eight million inhabitants, and some of the most penal drink laws in Europe. It also has a flourishing black market distilling and brewing industry, and since 1950, alcohol consumption has risen officially by 38 per cent. (The true figure is likely to be much higher, but the gentlemen of the black market are reluctant to take part in Government statistical reviews.)

In Finland, the Government not only makes the drink, but tries to tell the Finns where and when they can

drink it. This arrangement has fallen flat on its face – along with the one out of every five Finnish adult males who has been arrested for public drunkenness – and since 1950, alcohol consumption has risen by 191 per cent.

But in France, where any attempt to impose drinking restrictions would lead to a second revolution, and where bars and cafés are often open for sixteen hours a day, alcohol consumption has *dropped* by 20 per cent since 1950.

Admittedly, Finns and Swedes have to put up with a depressingly long winter. Admittedly, the Nordic temperament is more sombre than the Gallic character. And admittedly, the Frenchman will take a glass of wine instead of a dose of schnapps. Even so, even making allowances for the great differences between the countries, the evidence doesn't show that more drinking time leads to excessive drinking. If anything, the evidence indicates that it is restriction rather than free availability that leads to the desperate bender.

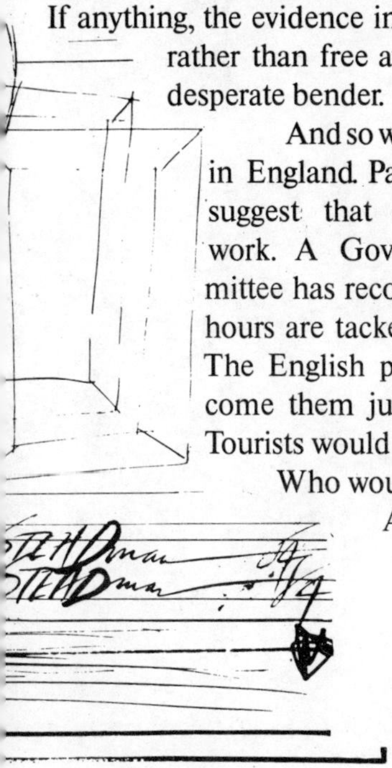

And so we have an odd situation here in England. Past and present experience suggest that drinking restrictions don't work. A Government sponsored Committee has recommended that a few more hours are tacked on to our drinking time. The English public would probably welcome them just as the Scots have done. Tourists would certainly welcome them.

Who wouldn't welcome them?

And why not?

Those against.

It's always tempting to damn with faint abuse the people who don't happen to share you own opinions. Meat-eaters lump all vegetarians together as the brown rice and sandals brigade. Capitalists are bloated. Socialists are rabid. Wimbledon umpires are blind in one eye. Cup Final referees are blind in both eyes. Every argument worth the name is made more lively and enjoyable by use of the verbal kidney punch, the slanderous accusation, the firm conviction that your opponent is a misguided dingbat incapable of seeing the obvious wisdom of your point of view, and beyond the reach of reason.

Unfortunately, the opponents of more flexible drinking hours can't be written off as a demented bunch of killjoys. This is not a cranks' gallery we have here, but decent people with genuine worries. We should point out also that they are not publicly calling for anything as fierce as national prohibition. However, it seems fair to assume that their reaction to a suggested increase in drinking time would be less than enthusiastic. Who are they? An inspired guess might include:

Alcoholism.
Action Against Alcohol Abuse
Lord's Day Observance Society
Scottish Council on Alcoholism
Alcohol Studies Centre

Education.
Teachers' Advisory Council on Alcohol
and Drug Education
Law.
Justices' Clerks Society
Probation Officers' Association
Medicine.
Institute of Psychiatry
National Association of Health Authorities
in England & Wales
British Medical Association
Health Education Council
Religion.
Methodist and other Non-Conformist Churches
Christian Economic and Social foundation
Church of England Board for Social
Responsibility
Women.
National Council of Women

The particular reasons for opposing any reform of our licensing laws may vary from one organisation to another. But their basic concern – the root from which all the particular problems grow – is excess.

Excessive use of alcohol causes trouble in the home, on the roads, in the courts, and wherever it occurs in society. But with respect to all the members of all those organisations, that is not the argument. Nobody would argue in favour of excess.

The argument is whether a change in the laws would lead to excess. Opponents of change believe that it would. Practical experience in Scotland shows that it didn't.

HOWDY, MAM..
SCOTCH AND AMERICAN.
TEN PAST THREE
PUB GRUB
ER.. MAY I PLEASE HAVE A DOUBLE SCOTCH WHIS—
YOU DEAF? TEN PAST THREE!
JEEZ... WHAT KIND OF COUNTRY IS THIS? YOU ASK FOR A DRINK AND THEY GIVE YOU THE TIME!...
Ye Olde Shoppe

Those in favour.

Using the same selection process – that is, by making reasonable assumptions rather than asking the various groups to testify under oath – a supporter's club for more flexible opening hours might look like this.

Agriculture.
National Farmers' Union
Hop Marketing Board

Commerce.
Institute of Directors
National Economic Development Office
Regional Chambers of Commerce

Consumers.
National Consumer Council
CAMRA

Finance.
City of London Analysts

Municipal.
Association of Metropolitan Boroughs
Greater Manchester Council

Tourism.
British Tourist Authority
English Tourist Board
Regional Tourist Boards
The National Trust

70mm
DOLBY
STEREO
THE
MAMMOTH PICT
GRAN
20 million over bu
2 hours too long,
and forty minutes a
closing time....

PRESENTS
EPIC
Alan Parker.

Trade.

The Brewer's Society
National Union of Licensed Victuallers
Wine & Spirits Association
Scotch Whisky Association
British Hotel, Restaurants & Caterers Association
National Association of Cidermakers
Association of British Travel Agents

And then there's you and me, the general public. Are most of us in favour of changing the laws? Who knows? Who asks?

Until there's a national referendum, which is less likely than a hot Christmas, the views and wishes of those most directly affected by the laws – that is, us – will remain a secret. A widely spread secret, certainly, shared by perhaps ten or twenty million souls. But not, it seems, shared by the 650 people in Westminster who represent us.

Never mind. News sometimes travels slowly. At least those of us in favour of change have the consolation of some support from these various groups. To be sure, when you look down the list you can see a little self-interest rearing its head here and there. But commercial gain is only one of many reasons for wanting to modernise a creaking piece of legislation which no longer serves the purpose it was designed for.

WILSON

**"It usually takes
a hundred years to make
a law, and then,
after it has done its work,
it usually takes
a hundred years to
get rid of it."**

An American, Henry Ward Beecher, made that observation in 1887. According to his timetable, the existing licensing law, a mere stripling of 70, has another thirty years to go.

If it does last that long, it's a safe bet that three things will happen: we will continue to infuriate tourists; the loopholes in the law will become bigger and more numerous; and the pub will become an endangered species.

The Tourist.

Tourism is big business. It earned us more than £4,000 million last year, or £12,000,000 a day, and provided 1,500,000 jobs – staggering figures for a small island with an unpredictable climate. It's big business in many other countries too, and becoming more and more competitive. Obviously, a change in our drinking laws is not going to make tourists rush to the Cotswolds instead of skiing in the Alps, or go to Margate instead of Marbella. But being able to have a drink during reasonable hours is a pleasant part of a holiday – as we know when we go to the Continent. It's also part of giving the customers what they want. What kind of business is it that *prevents* customers from buying something they want? A funny business indeed.

The Loopholes.

Strictly speaking, anything that can accommodate trains, boats, planes, clubs, wine bars, supermarkets and

CAMPARI SODA!
VODKA AND TONIC!
LEMONADE
BRANDY!
HALF OF SHANDY
BLACK
WHISKY AND GINGER!
SAME AGAIN!

DER!
ORDER!
ORDER!
GIN AND TONIC!
M AND
CKCURRANT!
TAN!
BACARDI AND COKE!
SMALL PORT!
DICKENS

Boots the Chemist in all his multifarious branches is a little too big to be described as a loophole.

A yawning chasm, a gaping void, a chink the width of the M1 – call it what you will, but to call it a loophole somehow doesn't do it justice.

The trouble is that the lawmakers of 1915 were not thinking of the future when they made their law. If your mind is fully occupied with the problem of getting those rascals out of the pub and back to the factory, you can hardly be expected to anticipate every crackpot invention and hiccup in society that might come along in the next seventy years. In any case, this is an emergency measure, for heaven's sake! Once the crisis passes, life will return to normal.

And so it did. Society made small steps – sometimes giant leaps – forward, leaving the emergency measure to age gracefully into a relic.

That's not to say the law didn't change. It changed to allow the consumption of drink on trains and planes. It changed to allow private clubs to sell drink at hours which suited their members. It changed to allow off licences and supermarkets to sell drink throughout the day and sometimes throughout the evening. And no doubt it will change again as life moves on. Progress is wonderful.

The one place it shows no signs of changing is at the local.

The Pub.

The appeal of the pub, and the basis of the publican's business, is that it provides not just alcohol, but a pleasant place in which to drink. It's a social centre, an informal club which anyone can join for the price of a pint. You can drop in to escape the rain, meet your friends, have a snack, read the paper, listen to some old buffer putting the world to rights, serenade the barmaid, ponder the meaning of life and generally have a relaxing and enjoyable hour or two. In formal language, it's a useful social amenity. And we'd better make the most of it, because the way things are going, the pub's future is far from rosy.

Proving arguments by numbers is often open to suspicion or downright disbelief ("there are lies, damn lies, and statistics"), but in this case the figures don't leave much room for doubt. Since 1967, more than 9,500 pubs have closed. Since 1980, more than 18,000 people who used to work in pubs have lost their jobs.

On the face of it, that might be a reflection of a change in our attitudes towards drink. Is jogging taking over from bitter? Has a cosy evening in front of the micro-computer replaced a game of darts in the local? Are we, for some reason, spending less money on alcohol?

Not at all. Drink sales are steady or rising in supermarkets, in off licences, in clubs, in wine bars – but the pub is obliged to close while the competition stays open.

If this goes on, it's not difficult to guess what will happen. More pubs will close. More jobs will be lost. It's as simple and inevitable as that.

What legal aid could do for pubs.

A change in the opening hours wouldn't automatically produce a sudden change in the pub's fortunes. Pubs do well or not so well according to the publican's ability to attract and keep customers.

What a change in the law *would* do is allow the publican to compete on more or less level terms with other licensed premises, instead of having both hands tied behind his back for a good part of the trading day. So there would be a fair chance – given hard work, decent beer, and a friendly atmosphere – of developing a profitable business with a real future.

First in line to benefit, for once, would be the public. Not just the regular, but the tourist and the occasional drinker; longer hours are more convenient. They also make it worth the publican's while to offer more variety in the way of products and services, from food to family rooms to live entertainment.

A healthier industry would employ more people,

and would provide a realistic small business opportunity for a couple wanting to set up on their own. At the moment, with an average of six thousands jobs being lost every year, you'd have to be either brave or daft to take the plunge.

Even the Government would do nicely. Nearly three per cent of all income derived from taxes comes from beer – about £2,600,000,000 a year – and beer is far and away the best-selling drink in pubs. If pubs continue to decline, so will beer sales, and the Government will lose out at the rate of 25 pence a pint. If pubs prosper, beer sales will revive, and the Government gets more pocket money.

So far so good, for almost everybody concerned. Convenience for the public, a more solid business for the publican, a shot in the arm for employment, and a well-filled wallet for the Government. All reasonable arguments for changing the law. But now we come back to the hot potato which has been tossed from hand to hand for years, and still seems as hot as ever: the prospect of the wild and uncontrolled drinking that might result from an extension of pub opening hours.

All right. Maybe it didn't happen in Scotland. But the Scot is a sensible fellow, not like that hot-blooded, excitable creature south of the border. Give *him* an extra few hours of drinking time, and heaven help us all! Lock up your daughters and barricade your home before he comes lurching out of the pub, crazed by mild ale and looking for trouble. Mark our words: there's no such thing as a moderate man after 10.30 at night.

The argument, of course, is never put like that, because nobody would swallow it. The phrase that is most often used is 'alcohol abuse,' which manages to be vague but at the same time infinitely threatening, like the rumour of an epidemic in the next street. Alcohol abuse does exist, and it is a sad and destructive business. But it is far more likely to take place in private than in pubs.

Quite apart from any moral reasons, professional

licensees won't tolerate excessive drinking; it's bad for business. Who wants to share the bar with a bunch of drunks? The Reverend George Brake, Director of the Christian Economic and Social Foundation, has said that the pub provides *"the most favourable controlled environment for the consumption of alcohol."* Any publican who fails to exercise that control risks losing most of his customers, or his job, or both.

Drink and the English.

It may come as a blow to our national pride, but one area where we don't lead the world is drinking.

Beer.

We come ninth, with an annual average of 195 pints per head. Top is West Germany, with 258 pints.

Spirits.

We come twenty-third, with an annual average of 7.5 pints per head. Top is East Germany, with 20.7 pints.

Wine.

We come twenty-fourth, with an annual average of 15.1 pints per head. Top is France, with 158.4 pints.

Our overall alcohol consumption is lower now than it was in 1900. So according to these figures, taken from *Beer Facts 1982,* we look like a nation of moderate drinkers. And you thought you were the only one.

CUSTO
HEATH

HAVE YOU READ THIS SIR?
BRITISH LICENSING LAWS

The fine print.

Most arguments about law take place on two levels. They start on the high ground of broad issues and general principles, and there they stay for as long as possible, because that's where the action is. That's where you uncork the telling phrase, the brilliant defence of your own position, the complete destruction of your opponent's muddle-headed point of view - *that's* the stuff which makes for great and stimulating debate.

There comes a point, however, when we all have to come down to earth and deal with the second level, which is nowhere near as exciting. Verbal tennis turns into legal shove ha'penny, and the letter of the law has to be defined in practical terms. It's all very well saying that everyone has the right to vote, but exactly how are they going to do it? And where? And should the ballot paper measure six by eight or four by ten?

This particular argument is no exception. Taking the two positions at their most extreme, you have alcohol abuse on one side versus the individual's freedom of choice on the other. The issue may be clouded by ambiguous statistics, loopholes in the existing law, and various red herrings, but what we're really talking about is quite simple: given that all freedom is subject to abuse, would this small addition to our freedom *be* abused? And the answer to that depends not only on human nature, but on the practical details of how any changes in the law would be put into effect.

This is what has been suggested:

- Pubs should be allowed to open at any time between 10 a.m. and midnight, providing they have obtained the necessary permission.
- Permission can be withheld or withdrawn at any time if the licensing magistrate feels that an extension is, for any reason, not in the public interest.
- Applications for extended opening hours would be made by the publicans, not by the breweries, and only by those publicans who wanted the extra time. There would be no legal obligation to extend opening hours.
- The law prohibiting children in pubs would remain unchanged.
- The present system of control – that is, the licensing magistrates – would remain unchanged.

And that's it. Very similar to what has been going on in Scotland since 1977.

Which brings us to perhaps the most popular word in the legal dictionary: precedent. When a lawyer is stuck for an answer, he consults precedent. When he wants to flatten his opponent, he quotes precedent. When he opposes change, he shakes his head and tells you that there's no precedent for it. Presumably, all precedents had to start life as informed guesses, but that's another argument. The point is that in this argument we have an entire *country* full of precedent.

The results of the changes in Scotland's licensing laws, as you may remember, were nothing spectacular. The public liked them. The police didn't find them a problem. The publicans either liked them or didn't bother to take advantage of them. There was, according to Lord Lyell, *"no significant increase in drunkenness offences or motor vehicle offences caused through drink."*

Even the most cautious lawyer – and there are few more cautious things in life, with the possible exception of the snail – even the cautious lawyer would have to admit that the evidence was mildly encouraging. Mustn't jump to conclusions, mind you, but it's just possible that the experiment worked.

There's no reason to believe that the same experiment wouldn't work in England. Nor is there any reason to believe that it will ever be tried, unless the people who make the laws are nudged into it by the people who live by the laws. And that's the general public, the silent majority, the man in the street, the average family with 2.8 children, the honest taxpayer. Yes, you.

"I guess mine host is trying to tell us something, Al."

"Some bugger's raising a fuss
two more Gin &

out the licensing laws again —
nics, George, please."

Dear Member of Parliament…

The process of making new laws or changing old ones is based on a series of ifs.

If a Member of Parliament wants to have a subject debated, it is put forward to the body which considers these weighty matters.

If accepted, it goes on the list of business to be dealt with in the House.

If debated, it goes to a vote.

If voted in, it goes up the House of Lords.

If blessed by the Lords, it becomes law.

In any 3 month session of Parliament, there might be more than a hundred subjects up for discussion, varying in national importance from an increase in dog licence fees to the sale of British Telecom. Competition for the House's time and attention is fierce. The dog licence lobby is baying over in one corner, the telephone lobby is wringing its hands with impatience in another, the pressure group in favour of crash helmets for bicyclists is limbering up, and there is furious activity on all sides because... *this is what we pay our Members of Parliament to do.* And the more effectively they represent our interests, the more likely they are to succeed in their own careers. Fair enough.

Not suprisingly, the special interests which generate the most noise and attract the most public attention–the vote-catching subjects–have the best chance of being debated. An ambitious M.P. is never going to make it to the top by sponsoring, let us say, tax incentives for puffin-breeders in the Orkneys when there are causes of more universal concern to be fought for. A big issue, something to stir the blood and make the headlines, a juicy conflict to set Sir Robin Day's bow tie a-quiver with excitement–*now* you're talking. That is meat and drink to our honourable friends in the House.

But here's a curious thing. There must be five million people who would favour a change in our licensing laws. (And that–forgive the political label–is a conservative guess.) These people come from all parts of the country, from all backgrounds, from all political parties, from all adult age groups, from all those socioeconomic pigeonholes that are so much loved by the

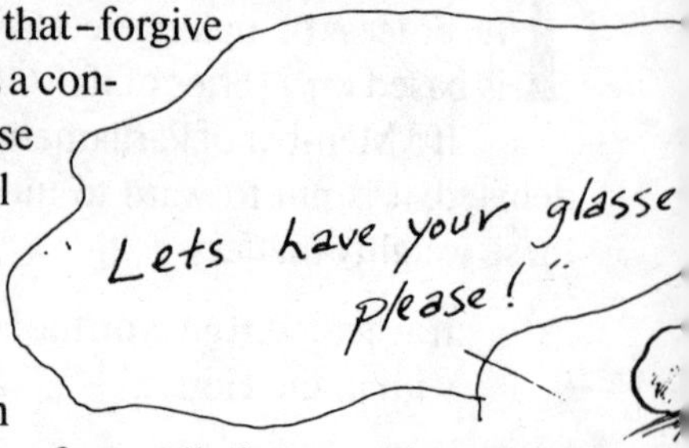

opinion research companies. A force to be reckoned with, you might think, a genuine cross-section of popular opinion. The snag is this: support for a modest change in the laws is so widely spread and unfocussed at the moment that the voice of the people is little more than a whisper.

Then there's the question of our national character. It's against our nature to be demonstrative about life's minor irritations. Your Italian, in the same situation, would get all worked up and chain himself to the railings outside the Pig and Whistle. Your Frenchman would park his juggernaut in protest outside Number Ten. But that's not our way. We don't make a fuss. We grin and bear it. We prefer the quiet grumble to the grand gesture.

Fortunately, even the quiet grumble can be effective. If there is enough mild dissatisfaction – *and if it reaches the right ears* – it somehow snowballs, winning promotion to the First Division and getting a new name for itself. It becomes "a groundswell of public opinion," and then it gets taken seriously. Groundswells are *votes,* to be counted in the hundreds of thousands.

Fine in theory. Where it falls down in practice is that we talk ourselves out of doing anything, for the worst possible reason: we don't really believe that one voice will make any difference. They don't need me. Someone else will sort it out. Anyway, I'm off to the pub.

Before you go, don't forget that there are fewer pubs now than there were a year ago, and there will be fewer next year than there are today. And once they've gone, they don't come back.

A vote for flexible hours could stop that happening. To start with, all it takes is a word in your M.P.'s ear, which can be found at The House of Commons, Westminster, London S.W.1. If you do it now, you can drop him a line and still be able to get down to the pub for a quick one before closing time.

NATURALLY WE HAVE DRINKING-UP TIME, MONSIEUR. IT IS FROM 8 IN THE MORNING UNTIL 4 THE FOLLOWING MORNING.

1 - 9 - 8 - 4